THE EVOLUTION
OF AFRICA'S MAJOR NATIONS

Egypt

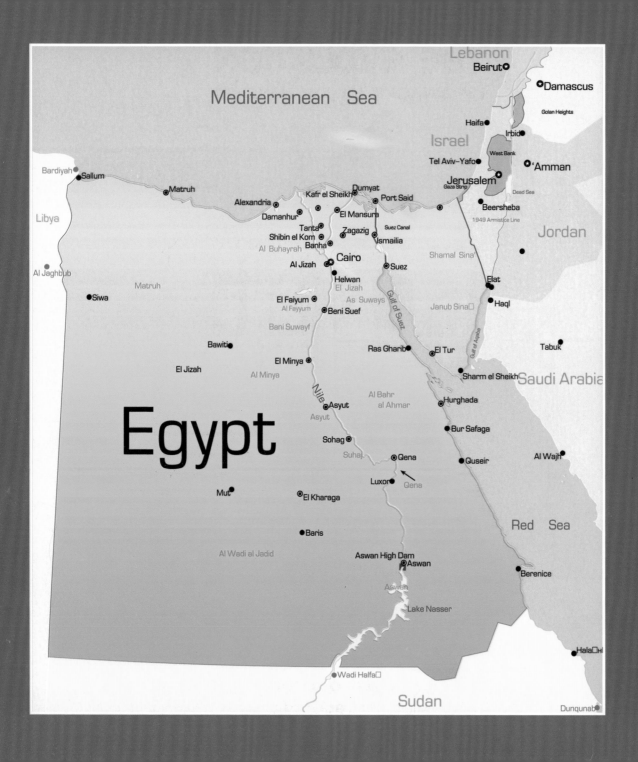

THE EVOLUTION
OF AFRICA'S MAJOR NATIONS

Egypt

William Mark Habeeb

Mason Crest
Philadelphia

Mason Crest
370 Reed Road
Broomall, PA 19008
www.masoncrest.com

CPSIA Compliance Information: Batch #EAMN2013-9. For further information,
contact Mason Crest at 1-866-MCP-Book.

First printing

1 3 5 7 9 8 6 4 2

Library of Congress Cataloging-in-Publication Data

Habeeb, William Mark, 1955-
  Egypt / William Mark Habeeb.
     p. cm. — (Evolution of Africa's major nations.)
  Includes bibliographical references and index.
  ISBN 978-1-4222-2178-5 (hardcover)
  ISBN 978-1-4222-2206-5 (pbk.)
  ISBN 978-1-4222-9419-2 (ebook)
  1. Egypt—Juvenile literature. I. Title. II. Series: Evolution of Africa's major nations.
  DT49.H213 2012
  962—dc23
                    2011018503

Africa: Facts and Figures
The African Union
Algeria
Angola
Botswana
Burundi
Cameroon
Democratic Republic
   of the Congo

Egypt
Ethiopia
Ghana
Ivory Coast
Kenya
Liberia
Libya
Morocco
Mozambique

Nigeria
Rwanda
Senegal
Sierra Leone
South Africa
Sudan and Southern Sudan
Tanzania
Uganda
Zimbabwe

Table of Contents

Africa: Progress, Problems, and Promise

Robert I. Rotberg

Africa is the cradle of humankind, but for millennia it was off the familiar, beaten path of global commerce and discovery. Its many peoples therefore developed largely apart from the diffusion of modern knowledge and the spread of technological innovation until the 17th through 19th centuries. With the coming to Africa of the book, the wheel, the hoe, and the modern rifle and cannon, foreigners also brought the vastly destructive transatlantic slave trade, oppression, discrimination, and onerous colonial rule. Emerging from that crucible of European rule, Africans created nationalistic movements and then claimed their numerous national independences in the 1960s. The result is the world's largest continental assembly of new countries.

There are 53 members of the African Union, a regional political grouping, and 48 of those nations lie south of the Sahara. Fifteen of them, including mighty Ethiopia, are landlocked, making international trade and economic growth that much more arduous and expensive. Access to navigable rivers is limited, natural harbors are few, soils are poor and thin, several countries largely consist of miles and miles of sand, and tropical diseases have sapped the strength and productivity of innumerable millions. Being landlocked, having few resources (although countries along Africa's west coast have tapped into deep offshore petroleum and gas reservoirs), and being beset by malaria, tuberculosis, schistosomiasis, AIDS, and many other maladies has kept much of Africa poor for centuries.

Thirty-two of the world's poorest 44 countries are African. Hunger is common. So is rapid deforestation and desertification. Unemployment rates are often over 50 percent, for jobs are few—even in agriculture. Where Africa once

The Nile, the world's longest river, runs through Cairo, Egypt's capital and one of the world's most crowded metropolitan areas.

was a land of small villages and a few large cities, with almost everyone engaged in growing grain or root crops or grazing cattle, camels, sheep, and goats, today more than half of all the more than 1 billion Africans, especially those who live south of the Sahara, reside in towns and cities. Traditional agriculture hardly pays, and a number of countries in Africa—particularly the smaller and more fragile ones—can no longer feed themselves.

The sun sets over a pyramid at Giza, one of three ancient tombs constructed at the Giza Necropolis site during the 26th century B.C.

There is not one Africa, for the continent is full of contradictions and variety. Of the 750 million people living south of the Sahara, at least 150 million live in Nigeria, 85 million in Ethiopia, 68 million in the Democratic Republic of the Congo, and 49 million in South Africa. By contrast, tiny Djibouti and Equatorial Guinea have fewer than 1 million people each, and prosperous Botswana and Namibia each are under 2.2 million in population. Within some countries, even medium-sized ones like Zambia (12 million), there are a plethora of distinct ethnic groups speaking separate languages. Zambia, typical with its multitude of competing entities, has 70 such peoples, roughly broken down into four language and cultural zones. Three of those languages jostle with English for primacy.

Given the kaleidoscopic quality of African culture and deep-grained poverty, it is no wonder that Africa has developed economically and politically less rapidly than other regions. Since independence from colonial rule, weak governance has also plagued Africa and contributed significantly to the widespread poverty of its peoples. Only Botswana and offshore Mauritius have been governed democratically without interruption since independence. Both are among Africa's wealthiest countries, too, thanks to the steady application of good governance.

Aside from those two nations, and South Africa, Africa has been a continent of coups since 1960, with massive and oil-rich Nigeria suffering incessant periods of harsh, corrupt, autocratic military rule. Nearly every other country on or around the continent, small and large, has been plagued by similar bouts of instability and dictatorial rule. In the 1970s and 1980s Idi Amin ruled Uganda capriciously and Jean-Bedel Bokassa proclaimed himself emperor of the Central African Republic. Macias Nguema of Equatorial Guinea was another in that same mold. More recently Daniel arap Moi held Kenya in thrall and Robert Mugabe has imposed himself on once-prosperous Zimbabwe. In both of those cases, as in the case of Gnassingbe Eyadema in Togo and the late Mobutu Sese Seko in Congo, these presidents stole wildly and drove entire peoples and their nations into penury. Corruption is common in Africa, and so are a weak rule-of-law framework, misplaced development, high expenditures on soldiers and low expenditures on health and education, and a widespread (but not universal) refusal on the part of leaders to work well for their followers and citizens.

Conflict between groups within countries has also been common in Africa. More than 12 million Africans have been killed in civil wars since 1990, while another 9 million have become refugees. Decades of conflict in Sudan led to a January 2011 referendum in which the people of southern Sudan voted overwhelmingly to secede and form a new state. In early 2011, anti-government protests spread throughout North Africa, ultimately toppling long-standing regimes in Tunisia and Egypt. That same year, there were serious ongoing hostilities within Chad, Ivory Coast, Libya, the Niger Delta region of Nigeria, and Somalia.

Despite such dangers, despotism, and decay, Africa is improving. Botswana and Mauritius, now joined by South Africa, Senegal, Kenya, and Ghana, are beacons of democratic growth and enlightened rule. Uganda and Senegal are taking the lead in combating and reducing the spread of AIDS, and others are following. There are serious signs of the kinds of progressive economic policy changes that might lead to prosperity for more of Africa's peoples. The trajectory in Africa is positive.

Egypt's monuments and natural landscape draw travelers from across the globe. (Opposite) The Great Sphinx is pictured in front of the Pyramid of Khafre, the only pyramid at Giza that still shows some of the original polished limestone casing at its peak. (Right) Men row a small boat down the Nile, the cradle of Egyptian civilization.

The Land

ENDLESS ROLLING SAND DUNES radiating the blistering heat of the sun cover most of Egypt's territory. The wasteland of the Sahara alternates between wind-blown dunes, rocky outcroppings, and pebble-strewn flats. This desert covers about one-third of Africa, and Egypt is located in its northeast corner. Egypt shares long desert borders with Sudan in the south and Libya in the west. To the north it is bordered by the Mediterranean Sea. And to the east it shares borders with Israel, the Gaza Strip, and the Red Sea. With a total land area of around 385,000 square miles (997,145 square kilometers), Egypt is roughly the size of Texas and New Mexico.

Despite its large land area, Egypt consists primarily of uninhabited desert. Over 95 percent of the population lives within a narrow strip of fertile land along the Nile River, or in the *delta* where the Nile flows into the

Mediterranean. The usable land in Egypt is essentially an area that is 9 miles (14.5 kilometers) wide and almost 1,000 miles (1,609 km) long. Cairo, Egypt's capital and one of the world's largest cities, is located in the north of Egypt. Traditionally, the area of the country south of Cairo is called "upper Egypt," and the area to the north of Cairo is called "lower Egypt." The names come from their orientation to the flow of the Nile, where traveling south is going up-river.

THE NILE

The ancient Greek historian Herodotus once said, "Egypt is the gift of the Nile." Without the Nile, Egyptian civilization never would have developed because the country could not have sustained significant human habitation. The Nile is the longest river in the world, stretching 4,187 miles (6,738 km) from its source in the lakes region of Africa. The Nile flows northward toward the sea—it is one of the few rivers in the world that flows south to north. The Nile has created a fertile valley running the length of Egypt, almost 1,000 miles (1,609 kilometers) long and dotted with farming towns and villages. The Nile Valley is the source of most of Egypt's food crops. North of Cairo, as the Nile approaches the Mediterranean Sea, it fans out into several *tributaries*, creating a larger fertile area known as the Nile Delta, which is heavily cultivated.

For centuries the Nile Valley would flood every year as snowmelt and rain in southern Africa increased its flow. The floodwaters were beneficial because they deposited silt, making the land more fertile. But the floods were unpredictable and often caused crops to be lost. During the 1960s Egypt built

In 1964 the first phase of the Aswan High Dam was completed. The second phase was completed in 1970, creating an enormous reservoir known as Lake Nasser.

a series of dams along the Nile, the largest of which is the Aswan High Dam. As a result, floods no longer occur, but farmers found that without regular silt deposits, the fertility of their soil declined. Today, fertilizers must be used as substitutes for silt. Additionally, the decreased flow of the Nile has allowed salt water from the Mediterranean to make more of the river *brackish*. Salt further destroys the soil and disrupts animal habitats.

THE DESERTS

On either side of the narrow Nile Valley lie vast deserts. The Eastern Desert extends to the Red Sea. It is barren, hot, and dry. At its eastern edge

THE GEOGRAPHY OF EGYPT

Location: northeast corner of Africa

Area: (about the size of Texas and New Mexico)
   total: 86,662 square miles (1,001,450 sq km)
   land: 384,345 square miles (995,450 sq km)
   water: 2,316 square miles (6,000 sq km)

Borders: borders the Mediterranean Sea to the north, Libya to the west, Sudan to the south, and the Red Sea, Israel and Gaza Strip to the east

Climate: hot and dry; mild winters; spring wind and sandstorms

Terrain: largely desert, with narrow a fertile valley and river delta

Elevation extremes:
   lowest point: Qattara depression, 433 feet below sea level (-132 meters)
   highest point: Mt. Katherine, 8,623 feet (2,629 meters)

Natural hazards: drought; wind and sandstorms; earthquakes; flash floods

Source: CIA World Factbook, 2011.

are the Red Sea Mountains, a north-south chain with peaks of over 6,500 feet (1,981 meters). The Sinai Peninsula, an extension of the Eastern Desert, is a triangular-shaped, sparsely populated area. It contains Mount Katherine, Egypt's highest mountain at 8,623 feet (2,629 m), as well as the Biblical Mount Sinai. Tourist resorts dot the peninsula's coast along the Gulf of Aqaba, and the Red Sea coast has also been developed as a major tourist attraction. All along the Egyptian coastline, which stretches for some 500 miles (804 km), resort towns offer tourists warm blue waters and a magnificent offshore coral reef.

The Western Desert, which is an extension of North Africa's huge Sahara Desert, covers over 60 percent of Egypt's total land area. It is, for the most

Tourists enjoy a vacation at this resort in Taba on the Red Sea.

part, a barren, sandy, and harsh environment. But unlike the Eastern Desert, it has several oases that provide water to sustain small farming communities. The most famous of these oases is Siwa, an ancient desert town known throughout Egypt for its olives and dates.

CLIMATE

Egypt's desert areas are often scorching hot during the day and bitter cold at night. They experience little or no rainfall. Cairo can be extremely hot and humid in the summer with temperatures of well over 100° Fahrenheit (37.7° Celsius). It can also reach a chilly 40°F (4.4°C) during the short winter season. Cairo, like most of the country, receives very little rainfall, but the climate is more varied closer to the Mediterranean. The large coastal city of Alexandria receives a fair amount of rain, and sea breezes keep the temperatures moderate.

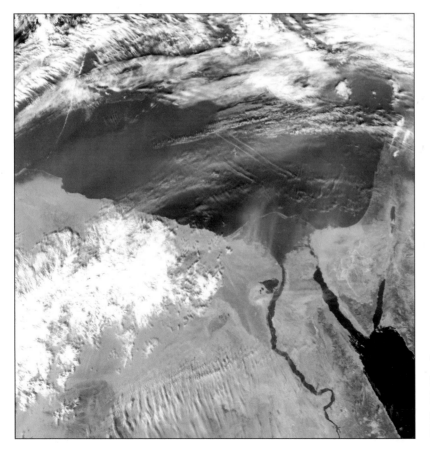

This satellite view shows a dust storm blowing out of Egypt and across the Mediterranean Sea.

A unique weather phenomenon in Egypt is the *khamsin*, hot spring winds that blow across the north of the country in April and May. These fierce winds can reach 90 miles (144 km) per hour, and they collect sand and dust from the desert, which they deposit in Cairo and other cities. The blowing dust and sand often cause respiratory illnesses in people and animals, and the high winds can damage crops.

WILDLIFE

Humans are not the only creatures to have been nurtured by the Nile river valley. Birds, reptiles, and small mammals have thrived in the harsh environment. Sometimes called the Pharaoh's chicken, the Egyptian vulture has black and white feathers and a bald, yellow head. Its tail is a distinctive wedge shape. Unlike other vultures the Egyptian vulture eats eggs in addition to carrion. They will use a rock to break through an egg shell, making them one of the few birds known to make use of tools.

The ibis was a sacred bird to ancient Egyptians. The sacred ibis species is now extinct in Egypt, although they live in other parts of Africa. They have a black head and some black plumage on the ends of their otherwise white wings. They have long curved bills, which are used to pluck food from the water.

The most famous reptile in Egypt is the Nile crocodile. It is the largest African crocodile and known for killing humans. Like all crocodiles, Nile crocodiles have four short legs, a powerful tail, and a tough scaly hide. They normally grow to a length of 16 feet (4.9 m), although some have grown to 18 feet (5.5 m). An average crocodile will weigh 500 pounds (226.8 kilograms), but some have been recorded at as much as 1,500 pounds (680 kg).

Unlike humans whose gender is determined by genetics, crocodiles have temperature-dependent sex determination. If the temperature of the nest is between 89.1°F (31.7°C) and 94.1°F (34.5°C), the hatchlings will be male. All other temperatures will produce female crocodiles.

There are an estimated 250,000 to 500,000 Nile crocodiles in the wild, although as desertification spreads, their numbers decrease. Since the building of the Aswan High Dam, Nile crocodiles have all but been eliminated from the Nile riverbanks in Egypt. There is, however, a growing population in Lake Nasser, the reservoir created by the dam.

The Egyptian cobra, or asp, is another famous reptile from this harsh land. The largest of the African cobras, it can grow up to 8 feet (2.4 m) long, and like all cobras, it has a hooded neck. The Egyptian cobra lives in semi-arid regions and is often found around humans. The venom of the Egyptian cobra is a neurotoxin, meaning it destroys nerve tissue. A human can die from a bite in about 15 minutes.

Cats are associated with Egypt for good reason. Ancient Egyptians domesticated small cats some 4,000 years ago, and most modern house cats are descended from those ancient pets. Many statues, bits of jewelry, and common household items depicting cats have been found in Egyptian tombs. Cat mummies have even been discovered. It is believed that the first type of cat domesticated by Egyptians was the sand cat, which first ventured into human territory in search of vermin. It is thought that the grateful humans took care of the cats in return for their pest control services.

In addition to cats, there are six species of canines in Egypt, including the fennec fox, wolf, jackal, Blanford's fox, Ruppell's sand fox, and Nile fox. The

Egypt is home to a variety of animals. (Above) Ancient Egyptians revered the Nile crocodile. The species was once endangered, but thanks to conservation efforts the wild population is currently estimated at 250,000 to 500,000. (Right) Egyptian vultures can be found in central and north Africa, India, southwest Asia, and the Iberian Peninsula.

jackal in particular holds a place of prominence in Egypt because the god Anubis was portrayed with the head of a jackal. Wild jackals eat insects, snails, fish, and farm animals, as well as melons and other fruit.

Many of the other mammals found in Egypt are either rodents or domesticated farm animals, like camels and sheep.

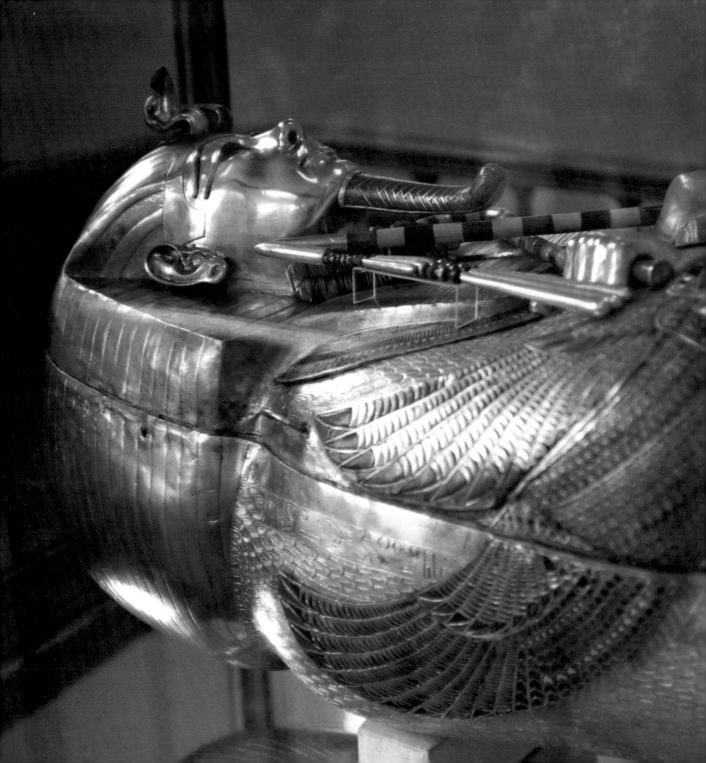

Ancient Egypt was ruled by a long line of powerful and extravagant pharaohs. (Opposite) King Tut's innermost coffin is solid gold, weighing 296 troy pounds (110 kg). (Right) This cartouche found in the temple at Abu Simbel is the hieroglyph for Ramses II, also known as Ramses the Great.

2 From Antiquity to Modernity

EGYPT HAS A LONG AND INTERESTING HISTORY. Egyptians developed one of the world's earliest civilizations and were among the first people in history to develop a written language, construct buildings out of stone, create a complex religious system, and form a highly organized society. Today, there is an entire field of history—known as Egyptology—devoted to the study of ancient Egyptian civilization and its contributions to the world.

People first began to settle along the banks of the Nile River in small village communities over 6,000 years ago. By around 3500 B.C. these communities had developed into two separate kingdoms: the Kingdom of Upper Egypt, stretching from the site of present-day Cairo south toward Aswan, and the Kingdom of Lower Egypt, covering the area of the Nile Delta. Each kingdom developed its own religion and its own pantheon of gods and goddesses.

Around 3100 B.C. King Menes of Upper Egypt unified the two king-doms and formed one nation. He established his capital at Memphis—near present-day Cairo—where Upper and Lower Egypt meet. The two religions were combined into one new religion. For most of the next 3,000 years Egypt would be ruled as one unified nation by a succession of kings, known as pharaohs, who were regarded by the people as divine figures.

EGYPT UNDER THE PHARAOHS

The early pharaonic dynasties—known to Egyptologists as the Old Kingdom—established a very organized and centralized form of govern-ment, employing soldiers, artisans, and priests. The pharaohs ordered the construction of magnificent temple complexes, monuments, and, most famously, the pyramids, which served as tombs. Ancient Egyptians believed strongly in life after death, and burial of the dead—especially of the pharaohs—was an important religious event. Egyptians believed that the dead should be buried with material items that they would need in the next world; thus, the burial chambers in the pyramids were filled with gold, jew-elry, and other items of great value that the pharaohs would need.

Around 2200 B.C. Egypt suffered a crisis when the Nile's waters did not rise as expected, resulting in lost crops and *famine*. People lost faith in the pharaoh, who as a divine being was supposed to control the flow of the Nile's waters, and the Old Kingdom collapsed in turmoil. A new series of pharaonic dynasties established in 1985 B.C. restored order for about 300 years. This era, known today as the Middle Kingdom, came to an end in 1650 B.C. when Egypt was conquered by the Hyksos. The word *Hyksos* comes from the ancient Egyptian term *heka khasewet*, meaning "rulers of foreign lands," and refers to a people that came from southwestern Asia.

By around 1550 B.C. the Hyksos were driven out of Egypt, and a new series of dynasties began, known today as the New Kingdom. During this era Egypt reached the peak of its power, wealth, and influence. Powerful pharaohs, such as Thutmose III and his descendents, conquered much of the Middle East, creating an Egyptian empire that stretched all the way to Mesopotamia (modern-day Iraq). Among the most famous pharaohs of the New Kingdom were Amenhotep III (1390 to 1352 B.C.), who built magnificent temples in Luxor; his son, Akhenaten, who established a new religion based on the belief in only one god (***monotheism***); and Akhenaten's son Tutankhamun (King Tut), whose tomb was discovered in 1922.

Following the rule of Pharaoh Ramses III (1183–1152 B.C.), Egypt went into a long period of decline. Eventually, Egypt was conquered by foreign armies. For centuries it was part of the Assyrian empire. Eventually, the Persians defeated and replaced the Assyrians and ruled Egypt from 525 to 332 B.C.

EGYPT UNDER GREEK AND ROMAN RULE

In 332 B.C. Alexander the Great defeated the Persians, captured Memphis, and seized control of Egypt. He also established a new city, Alexandria, on the Mediterranean coast. After Alexander's death one of his generals, Ptolemy, took control of the country, and his Greek descendents—known as the Ptolemies—ruled Egypt for the next 300 years. During this period Alexandria became one of the greatest cities in the known world. It was a wealthy center of trade and scholarship, and the ancient library at Alexandria

This Persian manuscript depicts the death of Alexander the Great. With his death in 323 B.C. control over Egypt passed to his general Ptolemy. Ptolemy's descendants ruled Egypt until the death of Cleopatra in 30 B.C.

was believed to have contained copies of every Greek text then in existence.

The last Greek ruler of Egypt was a woman—the famous Cleopatra. Although she was romantically involved with the Roman general Julius Caesar, she tried to keep Egypt independent of Roman rule. Eventually, Caesar was assassinated. Marc Antony took over ruling Egypt and summoned Cleopatra to him. As with Caesar, Cleopatra began a romantic relationship with Antony, using their connection to influence the political status of her country. Other Roman leaders were not pleased by Antony's actions and decided to bring Egypt under greater control. In 31 B.C. the Roman navy defeated the Egyptians. Marc Antony and Cleopatra committed suicide after being unable to defend Alexandria in 30 B.C.

Egypt was ruled by the Romans for nearly 700 years. Although Egyptians were given Roman citizenship in A.D. 212, Egypt was mostly exploited by Rome as a source of grain and taxes.

As the Christian religion spread throughout the Roman Empire, it also became well established in Egypt. At first Christianity was harshly suppressed by Rome, but in A.D. 325, it was declared by the Emperor Constantine to be a legitimate religion. Egyptian Christians became known as Copts, and eventually formed their own branch of Christianity—known as the Coptic Church—due to doctrinal differences with the Catholic Church. Today, the Coptic Church is still the dominant Christian denomination in Egypt.

THE ARAB CONQUEST OF EGYPT

The prophet Muhammad, an Arab merchant living in what is today Saudi Arabia, founded the Islamic religion based on revelations he claimed to have received from God, whom he called Allah. These revelations were later recorded in a sacred book known as the Qur'an. When Muhammad died in 632, his followers, called Muslims, vowed to spread Islam's message throughout the world. In 639 an Arab Muslim army crossed into Egypt, and by 641 the Muslims had conquered the country. They established a new capital city, Fustat, at the site of present-day Cairo.

Copies of the Qur'an containing hand-written calligraphy are often ornately decorated in colored ink with patterns called arabesques.

The Muslims gave Egyptians two choices: either convert to Islam or maintain their current religion but pay a special tax. Over time most Egyptians converted, but some chose to remain members of the Coptic Church and pay the tax. (Egypt also had a Jewish community, many members of which also chose to pay the tax.) Other than having to pay the special tax, non-Muslims were generally treated well. After the conquest Arab tribes began to settle in Egypt, and Arabic became the official language of government and business.

For the first two centuries after the Arab conquest, Egypt was ruled from afar by the *caliphs* (the supreme Islamic leaders) in Damascus and Baghdad. In 969 a Muslim *dynasty* called the Fatimids took control in Cairo. The Fatimids established a powerful Egyptian empire, which briefly ruled all of North Africa, Sicily, Jerusalem, and parts of eastern Arabia. But in 1099 the *crusaders*—European Christian armies seeking to recapture the Holy Land from the Muslims—defeated the Fatimid armies in Jerusalem and even threatened to capture Egypt itself.

The crusaders eventually were driven out of the Middle East, and a new dynasty came to power in Egypt: the Mamluks. The Mamluks, who were Muslims of Turkish descent, ruled Egypt from 1250 until 1517. Under Mamluk rule Cairo grew in size, power, and prestige. By the 14th century Cairo had become the religious and scholarly center of the Islamic world.

EGYPT UNDER THE OTTOMAN EMPIRE

In 1517 the Ottoman Turks, who ruled an enormous empire from their capital at Istanbul, defeated the Mamluk armies outside of Cairo and conquered

Egypt. At its height the Ottoman Empire included North Africa, the Arabian Peninsula, the eastern coast of the Mediterranean, and large parts of Eastern Europe and Central Asia. But the Ottoman sultans allowed local leaders to maintain control so long as they paid taxes to the empire, so for the next few centuries Mamluk leaders continued to have great power and influence in Egypt. In fact, during certain periods Egypt was effectively free from Ottoman control.

In 1798 a French invasion force led by Napoleon landed near Alexandria. The French, who were locked in a fierce competition with Britain to build a dominant colonial empire, saw Egypt as a great strategic prize. In 1801 the Ottomans, with help from the British, drove the French out of Egypt.

In 1805 the Ottoman emperor appointed Mohammed Ali, an Albanian by birth, as governor of Egypt. Mohammed Ali became one of the most important rulers in Egyptian history. Egypt was a major exporter of raw cotton, most of which was sent to Britain or France to supply those nations' textile factories. Mohammed Ali launched a campaign to modernize the Egyptian economy by building textile factories

As pasha, or ruler, of Egypt, Mohammed Ali built a strong military modeled on the armies of European countries. Because Ali needed money to run the military, he ordered Egyptians to grow cotton for export, and forced peasants to work in factories making military supplies.

and other industries to compete with the Europeans. His goal was to raise Egypt up to European standards of development. Mohammed Ali ruled Egypt for 43 years and is regarded by many as the "father of modern Egypt."

Mohammed Ali's grandson, Isma'il, took over in 1863 and pursued policies similar to those of his grandfather. He modernized Egypt's towns and cities and expanded public education. During his rule a company formed by the British and French completed one of the greatest engineering projects in history, the Suez Canal. When it opened in 1869, the Suez Canal connected the Mediterranean and the Red Sea, allowing ships to travel between Europe and Asia without having to sail around Africa.

Isma'il borrowed millions of dollars for his various modernization projects, mostly from European governments and banks. However, the country was not able to pay back these loans and eventually became bankrupt. Isma'il was forced from office, and a new ruler, or *khedive*, was placed in charge. Egyptians resented the new khedive, who they believed would do whatever the Europeans told him to do. As opposition mounted, British troops were sent to occupy Egypt in 1882 to put down the revolt and protect Britain's significant investments in the country.

EGYPT UNDER BRITISH RULE

Although officially Egypt was still part of the Ottoman Empire, the British actually ruled the country after 1882. British officials were placed in all the important government positions, and Egyptians had little say in how their country was run. In 1914 the Ottoman Empire entered World War I on the

A steamship enters the Suez Canal at Port Said, circa 1910.

side of Germany, against the British. Britain retaliated by declaring Egypt a British *protectorate* and severing it once and for all from the Ottomans.

Under British rule, *nationalism* became a growing force in Egypt. Many Egyptians began to demand full independence and the complete withdrawal of the English forces. Nationalist feelings intensified during World War I as the British forced thousands of Egyptians to join the army and fight the Ottomans. After the war Egyptian nationalists demanded independence from Britain; the British refused and arrested nationalist leaders. This led to strikes, marches, and violent demonstrations throughout Egypt.

In 1922, Britain declared Egypt independent, appointing a king, Fuad I, to rule the country and establishing an elected parliament similar to Britain's own. However, British troops remained in the country to protect the Suez Canal, and the British still had a lot of influence over King Fuad.

In 1936 King Farouk I succeeded his father, Fuad I, as monarch of Egypt. He was the first king to speak to the Egyptian public, using the radio to deliver an address after his coronation.

Soon after World War II broke out in 1939, the armies of Italy and Nazi Germany attempted to capture Egypt and the Suez Canal. The German Army was initially successful, but in 1942 British forces stopped their advance at El Alamein. The next year, an important conference between U.S. President Franklin D. Roosevelt, British Prime Minister Winston Churchill, and Chinese leader Chiang Kai-Shek was held in Cairo. In 1947, two years after the Second World War ended, the British pulled their troops back to the Suez Canal area.

The Egyptian army joined the armies of other Arab countries in attacking Israel shortly after that state declared its independence in May 1948. Although the Arabs were defeated, Egypt did gain control of the Gaza Strip, an adjacent territory on the Mediterranean coast.

INDEPENDENCE

In 1952 a group of Egyptian military officers known as the Free Officers overthrew the government of King Farouk and seized power. Their most dynamic leader was a young colonel named Gamal Abdul Nasser, who fiercely desired an end to all British influence in Egypt. The Free Officers abolished the monarchy and declared Egypt a republic. In 1956 Nasser was elected president.

Nasser and the Free Officers launched a major program to reform Egyptian society by nationalizing property and giving more land to the poor. They also sought to keep Egypt independent from both the West and the Soviet Union, a policy that angered the United States and its allies, which wanted Egypt to join their anti-communist Cold War struggle. Nasser's most ambitious plan was the construction of the Aswan High Dam, a massive project to dam the waters of the upper Nile to create more farmland and generate electric power. When the United States and Britain refused to loan Egypt money for this project under favorable terms, Nasser responded by *nationalizing* the Suez Canal, which was then still owned by a joint British and French company.

President Gamal Abdul Nasser led Egypt into independence and modernity. He became a hero to many Arabs because of his opposition to Western influence.

In response, Britain and France launched a military invasion to regain control of the canal. Israel, seeing an opportunity to seize the Sinai Peninsula from Egypt, joined in the attack. Although militarily successful, the attack against Egypt was condemned universally. The Soviet Union threatened a missile attack on Britain and France if they did not withdraw, and the United States pressured the Israelis to pull back to their border. Within two months the invading forces were withdrawn. Egypt took control of the canal and began receiving all of the revenue generated by canal tolls.

Nasser immediately became a hero, not only to Egyptians but to the entire Arab world. For the first time, an Arab leader had stood up to the Europeans and won. The Soviet Union took advantage of this situation and offered to help finance the Aswan High Dam. In return Egypt began buying military weaponry from the Soviets.

WAR AND PEACE WITH ISRAEL

During the 1960s Nasser became an outspoken voice for the liberation of all Arab lands from foreign control. He especially supported the cause of the Palestinians, who resisted Israel's existence in their homeland. As Nasser's anti-Israel speeches grew stronger and more popular, Israel began to fear that he was planning to attack. In June 1967, after Egypt closed the Straits of Tiran to Israeli commerce and deployed troops along the border, Israel decided to strike first. It launched a massive invasion of the Sinai Peninsula. Within six days Israel controlled the Sinai all the way to the Suez Canal. Despite the humiliating defeat and loss of revenue from the now-closed canal, Nasser remained popular and firmly in control.

Nasser died suddenly in 1970 and was replaced by his vice president, Anwar Sadat, who formed the National Democratic Party (NDP) that has ruled Egypt since 1978. Sadat reversed many of Nasser's economic policies

Egyptian president Anwar Sadat, U.S. president Jimmy Carter, and Israeli prime minister Menachem Begin sign the historic peace accord at the White House in September 1978. The peace agreement between Egypt and Israel has lasted to this day.

and opened the Egyptian economy to more foreign investment, a policy known in Arabic as *infitah*. He expelled thousands of Soviet military advisors from Egypt and indicated that he wanted closer relations with the United States. He also attempted, through U.S. diplomats, to negotiate an Israeli withdrawal from the Sinai, but to no avail. Because diplomacy had failed, in October 1973 Sadat launched an attack across the Suez Canal in an attempt to drive Israeli forces out of the Sinai. Initially, the Egyptian army did much better than expected and regained much of the territory they had lost in 1967. Quickly, however, Israel gained the upper hand, crossing back over the Suez and trapping the Egyptian Third Army where there was no access to food or water. There was nothing to stop Israeli forces from marching to Cairo. The dire situation led to a cease-fire agreement. By the time the cease-fire was signed, many Egyptians felt they had regained their national pride because of their early victories.

In a dramatic diplomatic move, Sadat traveled to Israel and addressed the Israeli Knesset (or parliament) in November 1977. Within two years Israel and Egypt had reached a peace agreement, with the *mediation* of U.S. president Jimmy Carter. Israel agreed to withdraw from the Sinai Peninsula, and Egypt became the first Arab state to recognize Israel.

Egypt's peace with Israel and Sadat's abandonment of Nasser's popular positions caused an uproar in the Arab world. Most Arab states severed relations with the country. Although many Egyptians supported the peace agreement, some strongly opposed it. The strongest opposition came from Islamic extremists, who believed that the existence of Israel never should be accepted and opposed Sadat's relationship with the West. In October 1981 Sadat was assassinated by a group of Egyptian soldiers with links to the extremists.

MUBARAK TAKES POWER

Sadat's successor was Hosni Mubarak, his vice president and a former air force general. Mubarak immediately rounded up Islamic extremists and put those connected with the assassination on trial. Mubarak maintained Sadat's ties with the West and the peace with Israel, but he also made an effort to improve Egypt's standing in the Arab world. By 1990 most Arab states had resumed normal ties with Egypt.

Under Mubarak, Egypt maintained close economic and political ties with the United States. The Egyptian president usually supported U.S. policies in the region. As a result, Egypt received more U.S. aid than any Middle Eastern country except Israel. Because of Egypt's pro-American stance, Western businesses and organizations were also willing to invest billions in the country.

However, Egypt under Mubarak was not a free democracy. After Sadat's assassination brought him to power, Mubarak declared a "state of emergency" in Egypt. This gave him broad authority to use the military, the police, and the courts to suppress any person or group he deems a threat to the state. Mubarak used these powers to repress his political opponents and maintain his position.

During the 1990s and 2000s, Muslim extremists attempted to weaken

Hosni Mubarak became president of Egypt in 1981. During Mubarak's 30 years in power, Egypt was been a strong ally of the United States. However, Mubarak was often criticized for using repressive measures to maintain his authority.

Mubarak's government through violent terrorist attacks against government officials, foreign tourists, and Coptic Christians. Mubarak was targeted for assassination, and survived at least five attempts on his life. The government responded by jailing thousands of Islamists and killing hundreds more in deadly shootouts.

THE EGYPTIAN REVOLUTION OF 2011

In late 2010 and early 2011, anti-government protests began to occur in a number of Arab countries, beginning with Egypt's North African neighbor Tunisia. The protests—which became known as the "Arab Spring"—were aimed at improving the political circumstances and living conditions of the Arab people. In January 2011, Egyptians began to hold mass demonstrations aimed at removing Mubarak from power. By January 29, it was clear that Mubarak's government had lost control, and the Egyptian army declared it would not intervene to stop the protests.

Mubarak attempted to disarm the protests by first firing his top ministers. He later promised not to run in elections scheduled for September. When these steps did not appease the protesters, he resigned as president on February 11, 2011, and fled the country. Commanders of the Egyptian military soon announced that the constitution and the parliament of Egypt had been dissolved, and that new elections would be held later in the year.

Although Mubarak resigned, the protests continued throughout 2011, as many people were worried that the military would attempt to maintain control over the government indefinitely.

On November 28, 2011, Egypt held its first parliamentary election since the previous regime had been in power. Turnout was high and there were no reports of irregularities or violence, although members of some parties broke the ban on campaigning at polling places by handing out pamphlets and banners. It appeared that Islamist parties had won the largest share of seats in parliament.

After the newly elected People's Assembly and Majlis al-Shura convenes in March 2012, a committee will draft a new constitution to replace the pre-revolutionary one, and then presidential elections will be held. The presidential election was scheduled to be held in May 2012.

Egyptians protest against the Mubarak regime in Cairo's Tahrir Square, February 2011.

At the start of 2012, Egypt's government was in a transitional period, with military leaders slowly turning over authority to newly elected officials. (Opposite) Protesters like these in Tahrir Squar helped topple the Mubarak regime. (Right) Field Marshall Mohamed Tantawi, head of the Supreme Council of the Armed Forces, has been de facto ruler of Egypt since February 2011.

3 A Government in Transition

SINCE PRESIDENT MUBARAK'S RESIGNATION during the 2011 revolution, Egypt's de facto government has been the Supreme Council of the Armed Forces, commonly referred to as the Military Council. The Council, which is chaired by Mohamed Hussein Tantawi, is intended to be transitional, surrendering its state powers to the president following his/her election, the date of which has not been set. In the meantime, the council has considerable legislative and judicial power, which has caused concern among many Egyptians that it will not willingly turn over control of the country to an elected government.

On February 13, 2011, two days after Mubarak fled Egypt, Field Marshall Tantawi dissolved the parliament of Egypt, suspended the constitution of Egypt, and promised free, open presidential and parliamentary elections before the end of the year.

In March, Egypt's prime minister, Ahmed Shafik, resigned due to continued protests. He was succeeded by Essam Sharaf, who served until December 2011. Sharaf resigned the position due to public opposition and because his power was checked by the Military Council. A former Egyptian prime minister, Kamal Ganzouri, was appointed by the Miliary Council on December 7, 2011. He had previously served in that position under Mubarak from 1996 to 1999.

U.N. Secretary-General Ban Ki-moon (right) meets with Essam Abdel-Aziz Sharaf, prime minister of Egypt, in Cairo, March 2011. Sharaf was forced out after just 10 months in office and replaced by Kamal Ganzouri.

On March 19, 2011, a constitutional referendum was passed in a public vote. It reformed laws related to the power and election of the presidency. The new constitution limited future presidents to two six-year terms. It also provided judicial supervision of elections, required the president to appoint a deputy, called for a commission to draft a new constitution following the parliamentary election, and eased the requirements for prospective presidential candidates to get on the ballot for national elections.

PAST EGYPTIAN GOVERNMENT

Since 1953, Egypt has had a *republic* form of government; its most recent constitution before the 2011 revolution went into effect in 1971. That constitution began with this declaration: "The Arab Republic of Egypt is a democratic, *socialist* State based on the alliance of the working forces of the people." The constitution was amended twice, in 1980 and 2005. At one time, the country's economy was centrally controlled by the government, with many social programs meant to help the poor. In the years since the ratification of the constitution, this economic policy has gradually changed. Anwar Sadat's *infitah* policies opened up the country to foreign trade. Both Sadat and his successor Hosni Mubarak also *privatized* businesses, making Egypt less of a socialist state.

Egypt's government has been described as a multi-party semi-presidential system. The multi-party system means candidates from many political parties can run for elections. All citizens over the age of 18 are required to vote, although fewer than half of the eligible population are registered. In Egypt's semi-presidential system there was both an elected president and an appointed prime minister.

While both the president and the prime minister ran the day-to-day operations of the government, the president was responsible for foreign policy and national defense. He wields the power to appoint anyone in the government that he so chooses but leaves the internal governing decisions to his prime minister.

Since February 13, 2011, Mohamed Hussein Tantawi has been acting president in his capacity as head of the Supreme Council of the Armed Forces. A national election for a new president was expected to be held in May 2012.

THE LEGISLATURE

The Egyptian legislature, the People's Assembly, was intended to enact laws, set economic policy, and provide for a national budget. Until it was dissolved by the Supreme Council of the Armed Forces in February 2011, Egypt's legislature included 454 members. Most of them were elected, although 10 were appointed by President Mubarak. The Egyptian constitution required half of the Assembly to be made up of workers and farmers, although this provision was not strictly enforced during the Mubarak era.

In 1980 an additional Egyptian assembly was created called the Shoura. Unlike the People's Assembly, the Shoura does not have the power to pass laws. It is an advisory council that reviews laws, constitutional amendments, and budget proposals. It had 264 members, 174 of which are elected by the people (the rest are presidential appointees). Half of the Shoura members were supposed to be workers or farmers. Like the People's Assembly, the Shoura was dissolved when the Supreme Council of the Armed Forces took over control of the government.

Volunteers check the bags and national IDs of people preparing to vote in Egypt's November 2011 parliamentary election, Cairo.

In November 2011, elections began to be held to create a new People's Assembly and Shoura. The voting process was complex, taking place in three stages spread over three months. However, turnout was high—estimated at 60 to 70 percent of eligible voters. Candidates of the Freedom and Justice Party (FJP), which represented the Islamist group Muslim Brotherhood, had won about 47 percent of the vote.

Another new political party, the al-Nour Party, won about 25 percent of the vote. The al-Nour Party represents Egyptians who follow the strict form of Islam known as Salafism. Salafis, as they are known, seek to return more closely to the form of Islam practiced by Muhammad and his first followers in the seventh century. Salafist groups have historically shunned public education for women and innovations like the telephone and television or any innovation not expressly permitted by the Qur'an.

In countries like Saudi Arabia, where Salafis are in power, all laws are derived from the Qur'an and harsh punishments are meted out to those who break the law. These punishments include amputation of the hands of those convicted of theft, or stoning of women accused of adultery. Women in Saudi Arabia are prohibited from driving or being in public without wearing a garment that completely covers her face and body. It is unknown what effect the al-Nour Party will have on Egyptian politics and social life.

THE JUDICIAL SYSTEM

The Egyptian constitution provided for a judicial system that is "independent, subject to no other authority but the law." The constitution goes on to describe the structural composition of the judicial system. The court establishment is called the State Council and is comprised of the Summary Tribunals, the Summary Tribunals of First Instance, the High Court of Appeals, and the Court of Cassation (Supreme Court). The State Council also oversees judicial appointments, which are made for life. Unlike the U.S. system of jurisprudence, which requires a trial by jury, Egyptian trials are decided by the presiding judge.

The Summary Tribunals are the lowest level courts. There are both civil and criminal courts within the Tribunals. These hear cases that have limited scope and small monetary claims. The Summary Tribunals of First Instance hear cases that have claims valued over 250 Egyptian pounds (or $43) and those that entail serious criminal acts. The Tribunals of First Instance are also the appeals courts for cases heard in the Summary Tribunals.

The High Court of Appeals hears cases that have gone through the Summary Tribunals of First Instance. Like the Tribunals, the High Court of Appeals is divided into civil and criminal courts. There are seven High Courts of Appeal, located in Cairo, Alexandria, Tanta, Al Mansurah, Asyut, Bani Suwayf, and Ismailia. Cases are presented before a panel of judges.

The Court of Cassation is the supreme court of the land. From a pool of 30 justices, 5 are chosen to hear a particular case. This court only hears criminal cases, and its decisions cannot be appealed to any high authority.

In addition to the State Council there is the Supreme Constitutional Court in Cairo, which is responsible for *judicial review* of laws that are passed by the legislature. Like the Supreme Court of the United States, this court only hears cases that challenge the constitutionality of law. Should the Court find a law unconstitutional, it is the job of the legislature to rewrite

Egyptians in the town of Hurghada celebrate news that Hosni Mubarak had resigned as president, February 11, 2011. Mubarak was criticized for using his position to enrich himself and his family.

their text. All of the decisions made by the Supreme Constitutional Court are publicly published in the Official Gazette so that the people may be informed.

CORRUPTION

Historically, corruption has existed at all levels of government in Egypt. The organization Transparency International lists Egypt 98th out of the 178 countries in its 2010 Corruption Perception Index. Corrupt practices of the Mubarak government are a large reason why so many Egyptians wanted to topple the regime in 2011. At the time he resigned, the Mubarak family's personal fortune was believed to be $40 billion to $70 billion.

In April 2011, Mubarak and his sons Ala'a and Gamal were arrested in the resort town of Sharm el-Sheikh and accused of corruption and abuse of power. In May, the former president and his sons was ordered to stand trial for the killing of some 800 protesters during the 2011 revolution. Mubarak, his sons, and several associates and government figures were also charged with abusing their power to amass wealth. The trials began in August 2011 and continued through February 2012. A ruling is expected in June 2012.

While there are anti-corruption agencies in place in the government, none of them have the power or autonomy to investigate or arrest suspects without approval and oversight from the president. Additionally, none of the government's recent steps do anything about corruption on the lower levels. They do not address police officers taking bribes or selling their credentials to others. They do not address thievery by public officials on the small scale. Because these levels of corruption are so close to the people, anti-corruption measures are considered as important to the public good as fair elections.

Egypt depends heavily on trade to provide food for its people. (Opposite) The Suez Canal, pictured here, allows ships to cross from the Red Sea to the Mediterranean Sea, so they do not have to sail around Africa to reach Europe. (Right) Many agricultural products, including vegetables and spices, are for sale in Egyptian markets.

4 The Economy of Egypt

EGYPT HAS THE WORLD'S 29TH-LARGEST ECONOMY, with a *gross domestic product (GDP)* of $303.5 billion in 2005, ranking just above Malaysia. It is the largest and most diverse economy in the Arab world and the second-largest economy in Africa.

However, although Egypt's economy is large, most Egyptians are not prosperous by Western standards. Egypt's GDP per capita in 2005—computed by dividing GDP by the total population—was $3,900, which was only the 148th highest in the world, ranking just below Suriname. By comparison the per capita GDP of the United States in 2005 was $41,800. Building a strong and diverse economy has been a major concern for Egypt's government.

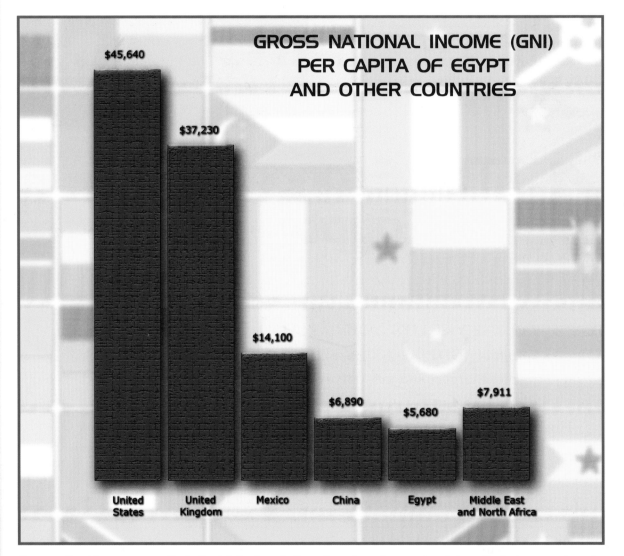

GROSS NATIONAL INCOME (GNI) PER CAPITA OF EGYPT AND OTHER COUNTRIES

- United States — $45,640
- United Kingdom — $37,230
- Mexico — $14,100
- China — $6,890
- Egypt — $5,680
- Middle East and North Africa — $7,911

Gross national income per capita is the total value of all goods and services produced domestically in a year, supplemented by income received from abroad, divided by midyear population. The above figures take into account fluctuations in currency exchange rates and differences in inflation rates across global economies, so that an international dollar has the same purchasing power as a U.S. dollar has in the United States.   Source: World Bank, 2011.

AGRICULTURE

For centuries Egypt's economy was based on *subsistence* farming along the banks of the Nile. A wide variety of fruits and vegetables thrive in Egypt's warm climate and irrigated farmland, and agriculture has sustained the population for most of Egypt's history. The cultivation of cotton was first started in the 19th century, and this crop quickly became a major Egyptian export. Many people still regard Egyptian cotton as the finest and most comfortable fabric in the world.

Egypt remains a heavily *agrarian* society today, and about 30 percent of the population is employed in agriculture. Cotton remains an important crop, and it is the country's principal agricultural export. Other crops grown include rice, corn, beans, vegetables, and fruits. Nevertheless, Egypt still imports much of its food, including most of its wheat. The Egyptian government has undertaken several large projects to expand the amount of irrigated land available so that Egyptian farmers can meet more of the country's food needs.

OTHER ECONOMIC SECTORS

As important as agriculture is to the Egyptian economy, there are other economic sectors that are more important in terms of generating *foreign exchange*, which Egypt needs in order to have money to import goods. Principal among these sectors are oil and gas; revenue from Suez Canal tolls; income from the millions of tourists who visit every year; and remittances from Egyptians living and working abroad.

THE ECONOMY OF EGYPT

Gross domestic product (GDP*):
$497.8 billion

Inflation: 11.1%

Natural resources: petroleum, natural gas, iron ore, phosphates, zinc manganese, limestone, gypsum, talc, asbestos, lead, rare earth elements,

Agriculture (14% of GDP): cotton, rice, corn, wheat, beans, fruits, vegetables; cattle, water buffalo, sheep, goats

Industry (37.5% of GDP): textiles, food processing, tourism, chemicals, pharmaceuticals, hydrocarbons, construction, cement, metals, light manufactures

Services (48.3% of GDP): tourism, government bureaucracies, banking, and finance

Foreign trade:
Exports–$25.02 billion: crude oil and petroleum products, cotton, textiles, metal products, chemicals, processed food
Imports–$51.54 billion: machinery and equipment, foodstuffs, chemicals, wood products, fuels

Economic growth rate: 5.1%

Currency exchange rate: U.S. $1 = 6 Egyptian Pounds (2011)

*GDP is the total value of goods and services produced in a country annually.
All figures are 2010 estimates unless otherwise indicated.
Source: CIA World Factbook, 2011.

While Egypt is not considered one of the world's major petroleum producers, it does have substantial oil and gas reserves in the Red Sea, the Sinai Peninsula, and the Western Desert. Moreover, discoveries of new oil and gas deposits are made every year, adding to the current estimate of nearly 13 billion barrels of reserves. While much of Egypt's petroleum is used for domestic consumption, oil and gas have replaced cotton as the overall principal Egyptian export, accounting for half of the country's export income.

Ever since Egypt nationalized the Suez Canal in 1956, all revenues from canal tolls have gone to the Egyptian government, with the exception of the period between 1967 and 1975 when the canal was closed due to the Israeli occupation of the Sinai Peninsula. The canal is a major transit route for super-tankers carrying oil and gas from the Persian Gulf region to Europe and beyond. United States naval ships also regularly traverse the canal. In 2010 Egypt made over $4.5 billion from canal tolls. In an average month over 1,000 ships pass through the Suez.

Tourism is also a huge industry in Egypt. In 2011 more than 10 million foreign tourists visited Egypt's magnificent historic sites, cities, and pristine beaches. Altogether they spent an estimated $11.6 billion on hotels, restaurants, and other services, making tourism Egypt's single largest source of foreign revenue. It is also a major source of employment, with around 12 percent of workers earning their income either directly or indirectly from tourism. Egypt's fascinating history, close proximity to Europe, and excellent tourism *infrastructure* mean that tourism will always play an important role in its economy.

Remittances, funds sent home by family abroad, are important to the economy as well. Several million Egyptians live and work overseas, many in the oil-rich Arab states of the Persian Gulf region. These *expatriate* Egyptians send an estimated $3 billion each year to family members and relatives still living in Egypt. These funds provide an important source of income for Egyptians, especially those in small villages and towns where jobs are scarce. Some Egyptians have become quite wealthy working overseas and have frequently used their income abroad to make investments back home.

The temple of Ramses II at Luxor, once completely buried under the sand, is now a popular tourist attraction. Construction of the temple complex began in the 14th century B.C. under the rule of Amenhotep III.

Ever since the rule of Mohammed Ali in the 19th century, Egypt has had a diverse industrial sector. Under Nasser, Egypt saw further rapid industrialization as he sought to make the country self-sufficient in many manufactured products. Among the products manufactured in Egyptian factories today are automobiles, textiles, iron and steel, chemicals, pharmaceuticals, fertilizer, and processed food. Many of these factories, however, are able to survive only because of government *subsidies* and high import taxes that make competing foreign-made products too expensive. Textiles are the only industrial product in Egypt that is a major export commodity.

ECONOMIC CHALLENGES

Egypt faces a number of serious economic challenges. Much of the country's food needs are imported from abroad, including over 50 percent of Egypt's wheat, 80 percent of cooking oils, and most of its sugar. The government provides subsidies to keep the prices of these commodities low, but these subsidies cost the treasury billions of dollars each year that could be used elsewhere. Given that many Egyptians exist on a very small income, however, the government has been reluctant to remove the subsidies. The only way for Egypt to become more self-sufficient in food is to expand the area of cultivable land. However, projects that would enable this are extremely expensive.

Egypt also needs to increase its exports so that it earns more foreign revenue. With the exception of petroleum and textiles, very few Egyptian products are exported abroad. And because of the need to import food and other goods, Egypt suffers from a large trade deficit, which drains money from the economy and hinders economic growth.

The Egyptian government is constantly taking steps to reform and improve the economy, often at the advice of the World Bank, International Monetary Fund, and other international organizations. In recent years steps have been taken to successfully lower the inflation rate, reduce tariffs on imported products, attract more foreign investment, and privatize industries formerly owned by the government. Some of these reforms have been painful to the average Egyptian, and the government has had to be careful to maintain social peace as it undertakes them.

The Egyptian government has passed measures to help small businesses like this pottery in Cairo.

A brick factory in eastern Egypt.

The underlying challenge facing the Egyptian economy is rapid population growth. Egypt's population has grown from around 55 million in 1990 to more than 82 million today. This rapidly growing population means that millions of new mouths must be fed and hundreds of thousands of new jobs must be created every year. It also requires the government to build hundreds of new schools, medical clinics, and other services every year. Until Egypt's population stabilizes, its economy will always be lagging behind.

Egypt is a land of both modern cities and old tradition. (Opposite) Alexandria is home to approximately 4.3 million people, a modern airport, and a busy seaport. (Right) Two Muslim women pose without veils. In Egypt, women can choose whether or not to wear a veil, although this may change if Islamist groups gain power through parliamentary elections.

5 Culture and People

WHILE MANY EGYPTIANS LIKE TO CONSIDER themselves direct descendents of the pharaohs of ancient Egypt, most modern Egyptians are, in fact, a mixture of the many different peoples and ethnic groups who have invaded or occupied the country over the centuries. The most important influence on Egypt came from the invading Muslim armies of Arabia, for they not only brought the Islamic religion, they also settled in Egypt and *assimilated* with the local population. As Cairo grew in importance as an Islamic center, many more Arabs from throughout the Middle East migrated to Egypt and eventually made the country their home. Egypt today is an Arab country, and most Egyptians consider themselves to be part of the Arab world.

Other important cultural and ethnic influences on Egypt came from the Persians, Greeks, Romans, and Turks, all of whom occupied the country for

THE PEOPLE OF EGYPT

Population: 82,079,636 (July 2011 est.)

Ethnic groups: Egyptians (including Bedouin and Berbers), 99%; other, 1%

Age structure:
0–14 years: 32.7%
15–64 years: 62.8%
65 years and over: 4.5%

Birth rate: 24.63 births/1,000 population

Infant mortality rate: 25.2 deaths/1,000 live births

Death rate: 4.82 deaths/1,000 population

Population growth rate: 1.96%

Total fertility rate: 2.97 children born/woman

Life expectancy at birth:
total population: 72.66 years
male: 70.07 years
female: 75.38 years

Religions: Muslim (mostly of the Sunni sect), 90%; Coptic Christian, 9%; other, 1%

Languages: Arabic (official); English and French understood by many

Literacy: 71.4% (2005 est.)

All figures are 2011 estimates unless otherwise noted.
Source: Adapted from CIA World Factbook, 2011.

extended periods of time. A small but influential community of Europeans—mostly from France and Britain—lived in Egypt during the 19th and 20th centuries, and many of their children intermarried with Egyptians. The port city of Alexandria, Egypt's window on the Mediterranean world, has historically attracted many foreigners, and in the 19th and 20th centuries it was one of the most *cosmopolitan* cities in the world. It was not uncommon in those days to hear Turkish, Greek, Armenian, and French spoken on the city's streets, as well as Arabic.

Egypt is also home to a few small minority ethnic groups, including Berbers or Amazigh, who live in the Western Desert; Bedouin, nomadic

Arabs who live in the Sinai; and Nubians, black Africans who live in the far south near the border with Sudan.

RELIGION

About 90 percent of the Egyptian people are followers of Islam. Most Egyptians converted to Islam soon after the invading Arab armies conquered the country in A.D. 641. Within a few centuries Cairo had become an important center of Islamic teaching and learning. Cairo's Al-Azhar Mosque and University, founded in A.D. 970, claims to be the oldest continually operating university in the world. It remains to this day a major center of Islamic theology, and among its graduates are some of Islam's greatest scholars and religious leaders.

Islam is practiced in different ways throughout the Muslim world. In some countries, such as Saudi Arabia, the religion's laws and traditions are strictly enforced. In Egypt, Islam is generally practiced in a less strict manner. For example Islam officially forbids the consumption of alcohol, yet alcoholic drinks are readily available in Egypt. There are even several factories that brew beer. Many Muslim countries require women to cover their faces with a scarf or other headdress when in public. In Egypt many women wear western-style clothes, and there is no requirement that they cover their heads. Nevertheless, in recent years more and more Egyptians have been adopting a stricter interpretation of their religion. Greater numbers of Egyptian women, for example, are choosing to cover their heads in public.

Before the Islamic invasion in the seventh century, Egypt was a predominantly Christian country. Today, around 9 percent of the population remains

Christian. Most Egyptian Christians are members of the Coptic Church, a uniquely Egyptian Christian denomination. Officially, they are not discriminated against by the Muslim majority, and many Copts have risen to high levels in the Egyptian government and in business. In recent years, however, Copts and Coptic churches have become the target of attacks by Islamic extremist groups. The government has condemned these attacks and taken steps to protect the Coptic community.

Pope Shenuda III, head of the Coptic Church, celebrates midnight mass for Orthodox Christmas, which occurs on January 7. About 9 percent of Egyptians are Coptic Christians.

In the early 20th century Egypt had a large and influential Jewish community, many of whom traced their presence in Egypt to the 12th century or earlier. Egyptian Jews lived primarily in the larger cities, and many were successful in business and government service. Most Jews fled Egypt after the creation of Israel in 1948 and Nasser's nationalization of private businesses in 1956. Today, only a handful of Jews remain, but synagogues still operate in Cairo and Alexandria.

LANGUAGE

Standard Arabic is the official language of Egypt and the language of instruction in schools. However, most Egyptians speak a form of Arabic that is different from the Arabic spoken elsewhere. Their particular language appears to have come from the city of Fustat, which was the Arab's capital city when they first invaded Egypt. It is unknown why the Arabs in Fustat spoke a language significantly different from classical Arabic, but their unique language replaced the native Coptic language as their influence spread throughout the country. Modern movements concerned with national pride wish to see Egyptian Arabic recognized as the official language of the country, since it is what everyone actually speaks. Some linguists even argue that Egyptian Arabic is not just a regional dialect, but is a separate language all its own.

In major cities many modern Egyptians also speak English, especially those involved in business or the tourist industry. In Cairo and Alexandria many signs and advertisements are in English, and English-language films are popular in theatres and on television. English and French have been taught and widely spoken in Egypt since the 19th century, and most

Egyptian school children study one or the other today. Because English is such an important language for international business and commerce, Cairo is filled with private schools that offer English language classes.

EDUCATION

Egyptian children are required to attend school for a minimum of nine years, but Egyptian public schools tend to be very crowded and often lack sufficient resources, such as textbooks, computers, and art supplies, which are needed to provide a good education. For this reason many wealthier Egyptians send their children to private schools. Fewer than 10 percent of Egyptian children ever graduate from college or university, and those that do often still have trouble finding a good job. Many Egyptians have complained that Egypt's colleges and universities are not doing a sufficient job in preparing their students in high technology, *white-collar professions*, and other areas that are needed for the country to compete in the 21st century.

As a result, wealthy Egyptian families often send their children to colleges and universities in the United States or Europe. A different option for some Egyptians is the American University in Cairo (AUC), which follows an American *curriculum* and has many American professors on its faculty. AUC is regarded as one of the finest universities in the entire Middle East. Many of Egypt's leading business people, scholars, and government officials are graduates of AUC.

Despite compulsory education for children, Egypt's literacy rate—the percentage of the adult population that can read and write—is only about 58 percent (for women, it is only about 47 percent). Most illiterate Egyptians are

Egyptian students pray in front of the American University of Cairo.

older citizens who live in rural areas. The literacy rate is expected to rise in the future because of compulsory education.

LITERATURE AND THE ARTS

Egypt has a rich literary tradition. The novelist Naguib Mahfouz (1911–2006) won the Nobel Prize for Literature in 1988, the first Arabic-language writer to receive this honor. Mahfouz's most famous works, such as the Cairo Trilogy, are sagas of family life in Cairo often set in the impoverished quarters of the city. He has been described as a master storyteller, and his books have been translated into English and many other languages. In 1994 Mahfouz was attacked and nearly killed by an Islamic extremist who felt that his works were an insult to Islam, but most Egyptians feel great pride over Mahfouz's accomplishments.

Music also plays an important role in Egyptian life. Street stalls sell cassette tapes of Arabic and Western music, and young people all seem to have small radios or tape players. While young Egyptians like to listen to pop music—both Western and Arabic—older Egyptians usually prefer classical Arabic music. One of the most famous singers in Egypt, and, indeed, throughout the Arab world, is a woman named Umm Kolthum. Although she died in 1975, her songs still are played on the radio every day.

The Egyptian film industry is the largest in the Arab world, producing dozens of movies each year. Egyptian-made films are subject to government *censorship*, but most of the productions are musicals and melodramas aimed to entertain rather than promote a political agenda. The popularity of Egyptian film throughout the

This recently discovered photo of Umm Kolthum was taken in the 1930s. Egyptian streets would be empty on the first Thursday of the month as people rushed home to hear her monthly radio concert. Her show could last six hours or more and consist of only a single song.

Arab world has made Egyptian Arabic one of the most widely understood Arabic dialects. American films are also very popular in Egypt, although films that are considered to violate Islamic principles are not shown.

CRAZY ABOUT SOCCER

Egyptians are big soccer fans. Whether in the narrow back streets of Cairo or in the dusty fields near villages, you can always find Egyptian boys playing soccer (it is rare to see Egyptian girls participating in sports). Every young Egyptian boy can name his favorite soccer team and player. Egypt's 14 professional soccer teams compete from September through May, and many games are on television. Cairo's two best teams—Al-Ahly and Zamalek—usually play before sold-out crowds in Cairo's huge National Stadium, which holds over 100,000 fans. Some of Egypt's best players earn large contracts with prominent European teams, and European games are frequently shown on television in Egypt.

Egypt's national soccer team has won the prestigious African Cup of Nations tournament seven times, most recently in 2006 (when it hosted the event), 2008, and 2010.

Cairo (opposite) is a destination for many tourists. It is a large, modern city full of office buildings and skyscrapers. Its name derives from al-Qahirah, meaning "the Subduer," referencing the planet Mars, which shone in the sky when the city was founded. (Right) The pyramids at Giza can be seen behind this camel rider.

6 The Communities of Egypt

EGYPT HAS A LARGE AND RAPIDLY GROWING POPULATION, and Egyptians are continually moving from rural areas to the cities. About 50 percent of the population lives in cities, and nearly one out of every four lives in the Cairo area. Although Cairo is Egypt's most important city, the country has many other interesting communities. In all, Egypt has 17 cities with over 200,000 residents.

CAIRO

Cairo is one of the largest cities in the world. Including the surrounding suburbs, its total population is over 18 million. Cairo is a sprawling city, and within its boundaries one can find some of the most impoverished slums in the world as well as sleek skyscrapers, elegant hotels, and fancy shops. Cairo is the political, commercial, religious, and social center of Egypt. It is also an important center in the Arab world; Cairo houses the headquarters of the Arab League, an international organization that represents all of the Arab states.

Cairo did not exist during the era of the pharaohs. It was established along the banks of the Nile in A.D. 969 by Egypt's Arab rulers. Much of the ancient city remains standing today, including hundreds of mosques, citadels, and monuments that are over 1,000 years old. One of the most exciting parts of Old Cairo is the Khan el-Khalili Bazaar, a huge open-air shopping area where one can buy everything from spices to gold.

In the 19th century a more modern area of Cairo began to develop, and it continues to thrive alongside the ancient city. The center of modern Cairo is Tahrir (or Revolution) Square. Within easy walking distance of the square are numerous government offices, the Egyptian Museum, the American University in Cairo, and dozens of elegant hotels built along the Nile.

The Cairo suburb of Giza, located across the Nile from Tahrir Square, is the site of Egypt's famous pyramids and sphinx. These ancient structures, along with Cairo's many other attractions, have made the city a major tourist destination.

Despite its fascinating historical sites and vibrant atmosphere, Cairo is not without problems. Principal among these are overcrowding and inadequate housing conditions. Hundreds of thousands of poor residents live in makeshift shelters among the mausoleums in Cairo's largest cemetery, a community that has become known as the "City of the Dead." Another serious problem in Cairo is air pollution from the thousands of vehicles that choke the city's streets.

ALEXANDRIA

Alexandria is Egypt's second-largest city, with a population of 4.3 million. Located on the Mediterranean Sea, it has been an important port city since its founding by Alexander the Great in 331 B.C. But Alexandria's most dramatic period of growth began in the 19th century as Egypt began to industrialize and ship more goods. Today, in addition to its port, Alexandria is home to many chemical, textile, and food processing factories.

Over the centuries residents have built new structures on top of old ones, and the coastline has shifted, causing parts of the ancient city to be submerged. As a result, many of Alexandria's greatest archaeological treasures lie underground or underwater. Archaeologists make new discoveries every day, but

The ruins of this Roman theater in Alexandria, Egypt, took 30 years for archeologists to excavate. Mosaics can still be seen on the floor and walls.

the city's most alluring secret—the tomb of Alexander the Great—has yet to be found.

Alexandria is also home to a modern monument—the Bibliotheca Alexandrina, a massive library and cultural center opened by the Egyptian government in 2002. Designed to continue the tradition of the legendary Alexandria Library, which was built by the Greeks in the 3rd century B.C. and later burned to the ground, the Bibliotheca Alexandrina will eventually house over 8 million books.

LUXOR

Luxor is located about 400 miles (644 km) south of Cairo along the east bank of the Nile. With nearly half a million people, it is one of the most important cities in southern Egypt. Luxor's principal industry is tourism. Next to Cairo, it is the most frequently visited city in Egypt, and for good reason. In and around Luxor are some of the greatest ruins of pharaonic Egypt. Just across the Nile from Luxor is the Valley of the Kings, a magnificent assemblage of temples and royal tombs where many pharaohs, including the famous King Tutankhamen, were buried. A few miles north of Luxor are the Temples of Karnak, an amazing complex dedicated to the gods of ancient Egypt. Most of the structures in Karnak and the Valley of the Kings are at least 3,000 years old.

Modern Luxor is a bustling town. The city has many hotels, most situated on the banks of the Nile, offering incredible views of the sun setting over the western desert. Luxor also serves as a market town for nearby farming villages.

PORT SAID

By Egyptian standards Port Said is a young city. It was founded in 1859 at the point where the Suez Canal—which was just beginning construction—entered the Mediterranean Sea. When the Suez Canal was officially opened in 1869, Port Said was the site of the festivities. The city quickly grew with the canal traffic, and today it is a busy center of over 600,000 people.

The Temple of Hatshepsut, located in the Valley of the Kings in Luxor, is part of a burial complex that includes the Temple of Mentuhotep II and the Temple of Thutmoses III. Hatshepsut was the first woman to crown herself pharaoh.

Port Said is a duty-free port, meaning that businesses may import and sell goods there without having to pay the customary taxes on foreign products. Every ship that enters or leaves the Suez Canal passes through Port Said.

Port Said suffered serious damage during each of the Israeli-Egyptian wars (in 1956, 1967, and 1973), but many beautiful buildings from the colonial era still stand, giving parts of the city a European feel.

A CALENDAR OF EGYPTIAN FESTIVALS

Holidays and festivals in Egypt reflect the country's strong Islamic identity, as well as its Coptic Christian heritage. Egyptians also celebrate several holidays commemorating important political events in their country's recent history.

Muslim Holidays

To determine the dates of religious holidays, Muslims follow a lunar calendar of 354 days, rather than the 365-day solar calendar. Although the dates of Islamic holy days are fixed according to the lunar calendar, they fall on different dates each solar year.

The **Muslim New Year** marks the beginning of the Islamic month known as Muharram.

Mawlid an-Nabi, the commemoration of the birthday of the Prophet Muhammad, is celebrated by prayer and often a procession to the local mosque. Families gather for feasts, often featuring the foods that were reportedly the favorites of Muhammad: dates, grapes, almonds, and honey. This holiday occurs on the 12th of Rabi'-ul-Awwal.

The ninth month in the Islamic calendar is **Ramadan**. Ramadan is a month-long Muslim holiday during which devout Muslims fast and pray throughout the daylight hours. It is the holiest period in Islam. As soon as the sun goes down, families and friends gather in homes for a meal denoting the end of the day. At the end of Ramadan, Muslims celebrate a major holiday called **Eid al-Fitr**—the Festival of the Breaking of the Fast. This is a joyous time characterized by feasts and family gatherings; children often receive gifts.

Eid al-Adha, or the Feast of the Sacrifice, is held during the last month of the Islamic lunar calendar, Dhu al-Hijjah. This holiday celebrates Abraham's willingness to sacrifice his son for God, and many Muslims commemorate it by sacrificing a lamb, which they share with the poor.

January

New Year's Day is an official holiday in Egypt, as in much of the world, although many stores and businesses remain open. Younger people and those who were educated or lived abroad may celebrate with parties, dinner, and dancing on New Year's Eve, but for most people it is a normal day.

Coptic Christmas is observed on January 7—two weeks after most Christians celebrate the holiday. In Egypt, Christmas is primarily a religious holiday and is celebrated only among the Copts.

March

The **Al-Nitaq Festival of Art**, held annually during the middle of March, is a weeklong celebration of art, music, film, and poetry. Events are held in the center of downtown Cairo, which takes on a festive air as crowds of people visit galleries, concert halls, and cafes.

April

Coptic Easter usually falls in either March or April, and, like Christmas, is principally a religious holiday. It is considered by Copts to be the

A CALENDAR OF EGYPTIAN FESTIVALS

most important holiday of the year. Easter is held on the second Sunday after the first full moon of Spring. For non-Christians it is a normal day. The first Monday after Easter, known as **Sham an-Nessim**, is a public holiday celebrating the beginning of spring. Egyptians celebrate it with picnics and outings.

May

Labor Day (or May Day), which the Egyptians, like much of the world, celebrate on May 1, is an official holiday. Schools and offices are closed.

July

July 23 is **Revolution Day**, a public holiday commemorating the Free Officers' 1952 coup that overthrew the monarchy of King Farouk and freed Egypt from British control. The day is marked by speeches and patriotic celebrations.

October

National Day, on October 6, commemorates Egypt's initial successes in the 1973 war with Israel, when Egyptian troops stormed across the Suez Canal and recaptured parts of the Sinai Peninsula. This public holiday is celebrated with military parades, official speeches, and events honoring veterans.

The **Cairo International Film Festival** is a major international event that showcases new films from around the world, with an emphasis on the work of Egyptian and other Arab world directors. Screenings and other events are held in and around Cairo's beautiful opera house.

November

The Cairo Opera House is the site of the annual **Arabic Music Festival**, a 10-day celebration of all forms of Arabic music, from classical to traditional. In addition to concerts the event is marked by conferences and discussions on the history of Arabic music.

Lentil Soup

2 cups dried lentils
2 quarts canned chicken stock
1 medium onion, peeled and quartered
1 medium tomato, quartered
2 tsp. garlic, coarsely chopped
4 tbs. butter
1 tbs. onion, finely chopped
2 tsp. ground cumin
salt and freshly ground pepper
lemon wedges

Directions:

1. Wash the lentils thoroughly in a colander set under cold running water. In a heavy 4 to 5 quart saucepan, bring the stock to a boil over high heat. Add the lentils, onion, tomato, and garlic. Reduce the heat to low and simmer partially covered for 45 minutes, or until the lentils are tender.
2. Meanwhile, in a small skillet, melt 1 tablespoon of the butter over moderate heat. When the foam begins to subside, add the chopped onions and cook for 10 minutes, stirring constantly, until they are soft and browned. Set aside off the heat.
3. Puree the soup in a blender or food processor. Return to the saucepan and, stirring constantly, cook over low heat for 3 or 4 minutes to heat through. Stir in the cumin, salt, and pepper. Just before serving, stir in the remaining 3 tablespoons of butter. To serve, ladle the soup into bowls, sprinkle with the reserved browned onions, and serve the lemon wedges separately.

Ful Medames (fava bean dip)

1 cup dried fava beans, soaked overnight and drained
2 tbs. olive oil
salt and pepper
1/2 tsp. ground coriander
1/2 tsp. cumin
1/2 cup lemon juice
2 cloves garlic, crushed
4 hard-boiled eggs, shelled
2 tbs. finely chopped fresh cilantro

Directions:

1. Place the fava beans in a pot, cover with water, then cover and cook over medium heat for 45 to 60 minutes until the beans are very tender, adding more water if necessary.
2. Drain the beans, place in a mixing bowl, and add olive oil, salt and pepper (to taste), ground coriander, cumin, lemon juice, and garlic. Mix well until some of the beans are slightly crushed.
3. Transfer to 4 soup bowls. Place a boiled egg in the center of each plate. Drizzle olive oil over each plate and sprinkle the coriander leaves on top.
4. Serve with pita bread.

Meat and Okra Stew

2 lbs. of lean beef or lamb, cut into cubes
2 onions, finely chopped
2 lbs. of okra (remove stalks)
5 tbs. of olive oil
2 cloves garlic, crushed
4 tomatoes, skins removed and sliced
Small can tomato puree
Salt and pepper to taste
2 tbs. chopped parsley
Juice of one lemon

Directions:
1. In a large saucepan, fry the onions in the olive oil until soft and golden.
2. Add meat and okra and sauté gently.
3. Add all other ingredients and enough water to just cover the meat and vegetables. Cook over low heat for 90 minutes or until meat is very tender.
4. Serve with rice and salad.

Orze Moumer (Sweet Rice)

2 cups of long-grain white rice
3 cups of milk
1/2 cup of sugar
1/2 cup of raisins

Directions:
1. Soak rice in water for two hours.
2. Drain rice, combine with other ingredients, and bake in casserole dish for 30-45 minutes at 250°F.

GLOSSARY

agrarian—pertaining to farming and agriculture.

assimilate—to blend in with another culture or group.

brackish—somewhat salty.

caliph—a successor of Muhammad as the spiritual leader of Islam.

censorship—forbidding something to be written or pronounced.

cosmopolitan—sophisticated and worldly.

crusaders—soldiers involved in military campaigns launched by European powers between 1096 and 1291 to regain the Holy Land from Muslims.

curriculum—course of study.

delta—the low-lying land at the mouth of a river.

dynasty—a succession of rulers from the same family.

expatriate—someone who chooses to no longer live in his or her native country.

famine—a severe shortage of food.

foreign exchange—the money earned from selling products abroad.

gross domestic product—the total amount of goods and services produced within a country in one year.

infrastructure—public facilities, systems, and services that are necessary for economic activity. These include roads, electrical grids, water and sewerage systems, telecommunications networks, and facilities like schools and hospitals.

judicial review—a right of the court system to review government legislation, and invalidate laws that the court deems to be illegal or in violation of the country's constitution.

khedive—title created by the Ottoman Sultan for the governor of Egypt.

mediation—the process through which a third party helps two conflicting parties reach an agreement.

monotheism—a belief in only one god.

nationalism—the desire by people who share an ethnic, religious, and/or cultural identity to have an independent state of their own. Nationalist movements emerged in many African countries during the 19th and early 20th centuries as a response to European colonial policies.

nationalize—to transfer ownership of a business, property, or industry from private individuals to the government.

privatize—to sell government-owned property or industries to private individuals or companies.

protectorate—a political relationship in which a strong state controls the affairs of a weaker one.

republic—a form of government in which leaders are popularly elected.

socialist—a political system in which all businesses, industries, and farms are owned collectively by all the citizens and are controlled by the government.

subsidy—a grant of money from the government to help people or businesses pay expenses.

subsistence—the minimum necessary to support life.

tributaries—streams or small rivers that feed into a larger river.

white-collar professions—jobs that typically require a higher level of education and do not involve manual labor.

PROJECT AND REPORT IDEAS

Learn About the Pyramids

The pyramids of Egypt are among the world's greatest wonders. Investigate how they were built and how long this took. Make a poster or diagram that shows the secret inner passages of the pyramids and where priceless valuables were hidden from robbers. Or build a model of the pyramids using clay.

Timeline of Ancient Egypt

Using a long sheet of rolled paper make a timeline of ancient Egypt, giving the names and dates of rule of each of the major pharaohs. Decorate the timeline with hieroglyphics, pictures of the pharaohs, and scenes of Egypt.

Crafts

Write your name and the names of your classmates in hieroglyphics. Check out a book on hieroglyphics or visit a web site—an excellent one is www.greatscott.com/hiero—to learn how to translate our letters into hieroglyphics.

Using gold colored construction paper and black markers, make a cartouche—a nameplate traditionally made of gold with a person's name etched in hieroglyphics. For help, visit www.harcourtschool.com/activity/cartouche/cartouche.html.

The Nile

Prepare a map of the Nile River from its source in the lakes region of Africa to the delta in Egypt where it empties into the Mediterranean.

- How many countries does the Nile pass through?

- What major cities are located along the Nile?

- Where is the Aswan High Dam?

- Collect facts about the Nile, including its length and the total volume of water that flows from the Nile into the sea.

CHRONOLOGY

c. 3300 B.C.:	Beginning of pharaonic dynasties.
c. 2575 B.C.:	Old Kingdom begins.
2560 B.C.:	Great pyramid at Giza is completed.
1985 B.C.:	The Middle Kingdom begins.
1650 B.C.:	The Hyksos conquer Egypt.
1550 B.C.:	The New Kingdom begins.
525 B.C.:	Persian occupation ends pharaonic rule.
332 B.C.:	Alexander the Great conquers Egypt, begins era of Greek rule.
30 B.C.:	Egypt becomes part of the Roman Empire.
A.D. 330:	Emperor Constantine establishes a new Roman capital at Constantinople. When the Roman Empire is split in two, Egypt falls under control of the Byzantine (Eastern Roman) Empire, based in Constantinople.
641:	Muslim Arabs conquer Egypt.
969:	Fatimid dynasty takes over rule in Egypt.
1099:	Fatimids lose a war to European crusaders in Jerusalem.
1250:	Mamluks take over control of Egypt.
1517:	Ottoman Turks take control of Egypt.
1798:	Napoleon and the French briefly occupy Egypt.
1805:	Mohammed Ali takes control of Egypt. He begins to modernize the country.
1863:	Isma'il Pasha becomes khedive in Egypt.
1869:	Suez Canal opens to traffic.
1914:	Official end of Ottoman rule and establishment of British protectorate.

1952:	Free Officers seize power and end British control.
1956:	Israel, Britain, and France attack Egypt but are forced by the United States and others to withdraw.
1967:	In the Six Day War with Israel, Egypt loses Sinai Peninsula.
1973:	In the October War, Egypt regains parts of Sinai and initiates peace talks with Israel.
1979:	Egypt and Israel sign peace treaty.
1981:	Egyptian president Sadat is assassinated; Hosni Mubarak becomes president.
1991:	Egypt sends troops to assist United States in Gulf War.
2003:	Egypt opposes U.S. war against Saddam Hussein in Iraq; the ruling National Democratic Party announces it will undertake political and economic reforms.
2005:	Egypt holds its first multiparty election for president.
2006:	President Mubarak meets with Saudi King Abdullah to discuss the Israeli-Palestinian problem.
2007:	Egypt's top Islamic scholar issues a *fatwa* (religious ruling) that permits Muslim countries to elect women as the head of state.
2011:	On January 25, widespread protests against the Mubarak regime begin; on February 11, Mubarak resigns as president; in November, new parliamentary elections are held.
2012:	Presidential elections are scheduled to be held in May.

FURTHER READING/INTERNET RESOURCES

Al Aswany, Alaa. *On the State of Egypt: What Made the Revolution Inevitable*. New York: Vintage, 2011.

Aykroyd, Clarissa. *Egypt*. Philadelphia: Mason Crest Publishers, 2009.

Chrisp, Peter. *Ancient Egypt Revealed*. New York: DK Publishing, 2002.

Firestone, Matthew, and Michael Benanav. *Lonely Planet Egypt*. Oakland: Lonely Planet Publications, 2010.

Osman, Tarek. *Egypt on the Brink: From the Rise of Nasser to the Fall of Mubarak*. New Haven, Conn.: Yale University Press, 2011.

Shaw, Ian, ed. *The Oxford Illustrated History of Ancient Egypt*. New York: Oxford University Press, 2004.

Travel Information

http://www.touregypt.net
http://www.egyptvoyager.com
http://www.egypttourism.org

History and Geography

http://www.arab.net/egypt/
http://www.ancient-egypt.org
http://www.egyptianmuseum.gov.eg

Economic and Political Information

http://en.wikipedia.org/wiki/Politics_of_Egypt/
http://www.egypttoday.com
http://www.sis.gov.eg

Culture and Festivals

http://touregypt.net/Culture.htm
http://www.bibalex.org

Embassy of Egypt
3521 International Court, NW
Washington, DC 20008
Tel: (202) 895-5400
Fax: (202) 244-4319
E-mail: embassy@egyptembdc.org
Website: http://egyptembassy.net

United States Embassy in Egypt
8 Kamal El Din Salah St.
Garden City, Cairo, Egypt
Tel: 011-20-2-797-3300
Fax: 011-20-2-797-3200
E-mail: consularcairo@state.gov
Website: http://cairo.usembassy.gov

American Chamber of Commerce in Egypt
33 Soliman Abaza Street
Dokki-Giza
Cairo, Egypt
Tel: 011-20-2-338-1050
Fax: 011-20-2-338-1060
E-mail: info@amcham.org.eg
Website: http://www.amcham.org.eg

INDEX

Numbers in **bold italic** refer to captions.

CONTRIBUTORS/PICTURE CREDITS

Professor Robert I. Rotberg is Director of the Program on Intrastate Conflict and Conflict Resolution at the Kennedy School, Harvard University, and President of the World Peace Foundation. He is the author of a number of books and articles on Africa, including *A Political History of Tropical Africa* and *Ending Autocracy, Enabling Democracy: The Tribulations of Southern Africa.*

William Mark Habeeb is an international consultant and adjunct associate professor of conflict management at Georgetown University's School of Foreign Service. He has counseled governments and businesses on issues related to Africa and the Middle East, and is the author of several books, including *Polity and Society in Contemporary North Africa.*